P9-DDW-088

Featured Tiny Thinkers:
Morgan Sealey
Benjamin Dulock

Ada Wants to Fly
A Tiny Thinkers Book

Written by: M.J. Mouton
Illustrated by: Jezreel S. Cuevas
Edited by: Amanda N. Franquet

©2019 Published by
Tiny Thinkers Books
All rights reserved. Unauthorized duplication of this book is prohibited by law.

Art Consultant: Deanie Mouton
Book Design: Amanda N. Franquet

Printed in China

US Library of Congress
ISBN: 978-0-9983147-3-0

Hi, I'm Hitch!

I've spent time with some amazing Tiny Thinkers! Join me as we learn about people and the science they discovered. And see if you can spot me along the way, as I tell you the story of Ada's real-life adventure that changed the world!

ADA
WANTS TO FLY

Written by M.J. Mouton   Illustrated by Jezreel S. Cuevas

A Foreword by
Dr. Martina Anzaghe

I am a scientist and I love my job: Asking questions, making guesses, and finding out how things work. I have the chance to discover something new every day. But what actually makes it count is: I can share what I've learned!

Giving lectures and teaching my students allows me to share my passion with others.

Besides my work, I am also the mom of two boys. I try to inspire them to ask questions too. Each day, I encourage them to do things that make the world a little better.

I was in school, like Ada and my kids, when I realized my fascination with science. I wanted to fight against viral infections and become a professor. I always wanted to save the world!

When Ada realized her fascination with science she followed her passion. Ada wanted to discover the world! She dreamed about flying, and studied birds. Ada made plans for a flying machine when she was only 12 years old.

Later, her studies helped to develop the first computer. Today, Ada is known as the first programmer. Ada loved what she did and left footprints for us.

Be like Ada! Follow your passion, believe in yourself, inspire others, and take the chance to leave some footprints, too!

"Where will I go today?" asked Ada,
as she was dreaming about flying.
"I can fly with wings, or a kite,
or whatever is worth trying."

"If I could fly, then I would go almost anywhere. Where shall I go? If I am flying, who cares?"

"I could fly over mountains, and rivers, and valleys, over beautiful fields with the fireflies in prairies."

"I could fly so far away that no one would be near me."

"I could fly like a sparrow, I could fly like a bee."

Ada was not happy just thinking about things.
She was determined to fly.
She wanted her own
wings!

"My imagination alone won't get me out of bed, so I will study the birds," is what Ada said.

Flying List

    1. Where will I go?

Paris, Rome, China, America, Norway, Iceland

    2. How can I build a winged machine?

Feathers, Yarn, Wire, Paper, Wood, Sprockets

    3. Why should I fly?

To go anywhere, See everything, Adventure, Danger

    4. How do I do it?

Study birds, Physics, try, try, try! Flying Horse?

She wrote down all of the items she
thought she needed to travel.
"What wings could stay together?
What could unravel?"

"Do I need feathers or silk fabrics for this flying contraption?
I can wire them together just to see what will happen."

She made a book on flying, for the whole world to see.
"Should I call it *How to Fly*, or *Flying with Me*?"

The name needed to be something quite clever,
about things that can fly in all types of weather.

"It does have birds so maybe *Flying Ornithology*.
I studied the birds' bodies so maybe *Flying Biology*."

"*Flyology*: a book of dreams about what is needed to fly, full of much needed answers, so you never ask, 'Why?'"

"It has charts, compasses, and details about flying.
It is a book about imagination and the effort of trying."

"To fly over mountains , rivers, or valleys.
To fly over cities with buildings and alleys."

NORTH
AMERICA

"I would certainly fly
to see places so far.
I just have to try,
but sometimes trying
seems hard."

AFRICA

SOUTH
AMERICA

Maybe you too can write a book about something you like.

Maybe a book about dancing, or swimming, or riding a bike.

Your imagination might want to do something more daring,

like wrestle a bear with some candy that he is not sharing.

Bearology

1. Can I wrestle a bear?   Sure I can!

2. How will I wrestle a bear?   I don't know.

3. Will the bear eat me?   Probably.

4. Should I wrestle a bear?   Probably not.

Ada Lovelace is famous for another reason that a curious imagination could only succeed in.

Every idea she had, and what she learned every step of the way, helped her give us a gift that we all use today.

We surely should thank Ada for following her dreams.

She was the first person ever to program a machine.

Ada grew up to be known as...

Ada Lovelace
1815-1852

Who Made *Flyology*?

Ada Lovelace was born on December 10, 1815. Her mother encouraged her to learn mathematics and logic.

Ada was often ill, beginning in early childhood. When she was eight, she was paralyzed after a bout of measles and spent a year in bed. Ada was eventually able to walk with crutches.

At age 12, Ada decided that she wanted to fly. In February 1828, Ada began to construct wings. She investigated different materials and sizes. She examined the anatomy of birds to determine the right proportion between the wings and the body. Ada wrote a book called *Flyology*.

Flyology was filled with examples of what was needed to fly across the country. Ada used the math skills that she learned at an early age in her future work.

She worked on Charles Babbage's early mechanical general-purpose computer, the Analytical Engine.

Ada Lovelace is considered the writer of the first computer program.